A Step by Step Guide
CogAT – Form 7
(Cognitive Abilities Test)

NUMBER
ANALOGIES

Grade 2
By MindMine

ADDITION

NUMBER ANALOGIES - **ADDITION**

Analogy

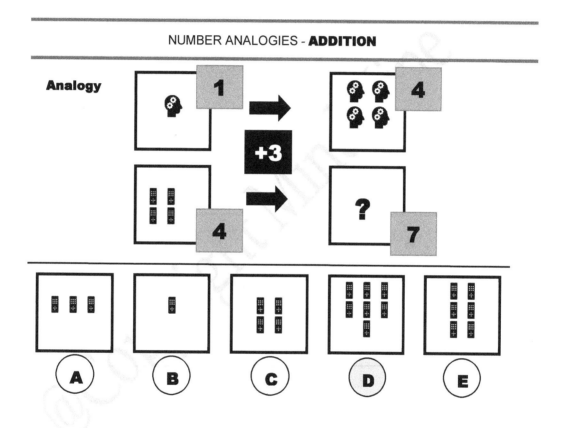

Analogy: Add 3	Given 1+**3** = 4 so 4+**3** = 7 **Answer = D**

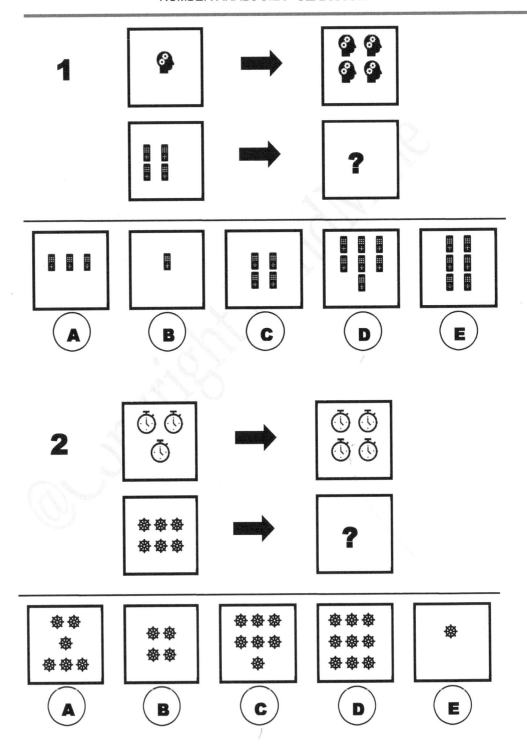

NUMBER ANALOGIES - **ADDITION**

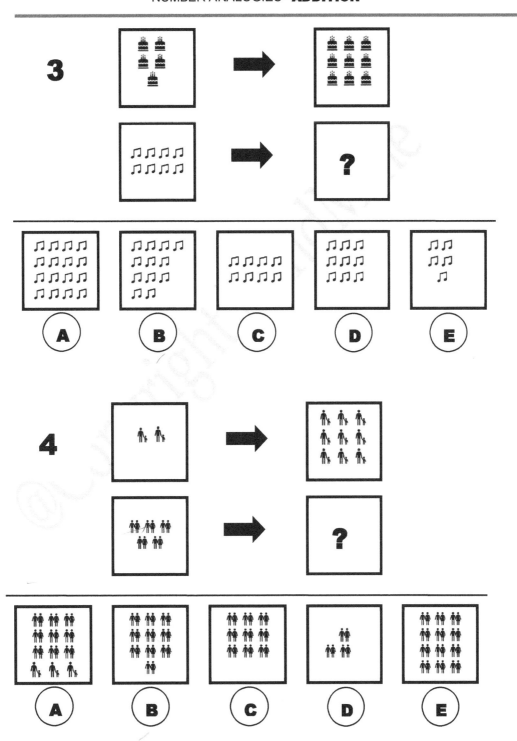

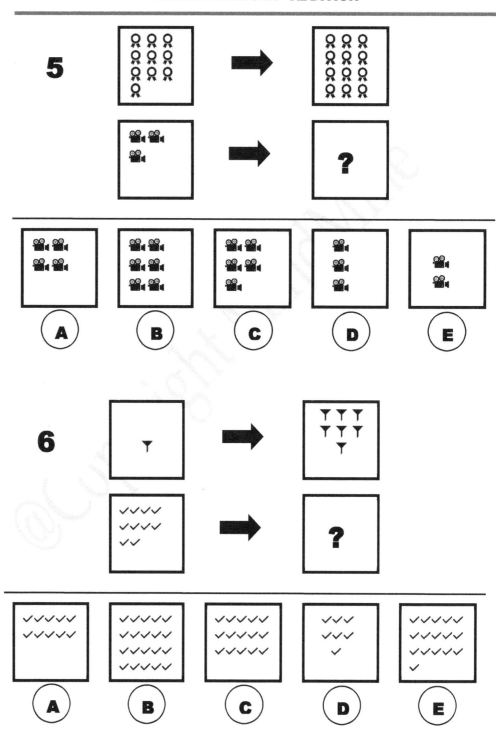

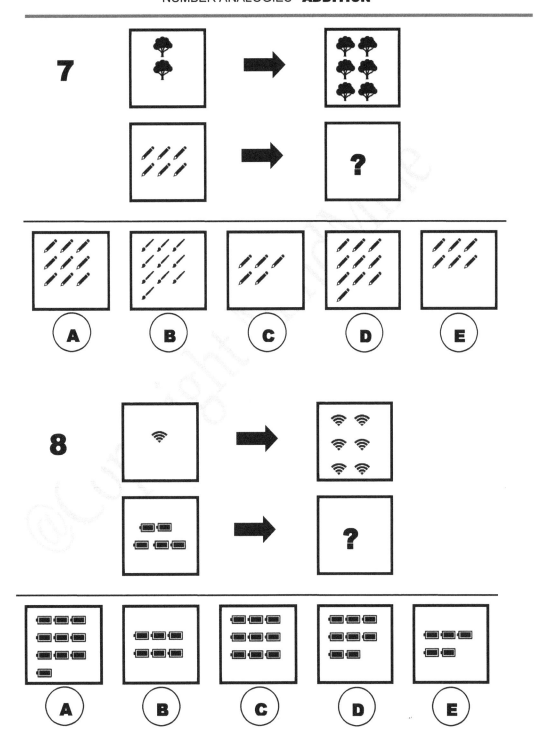

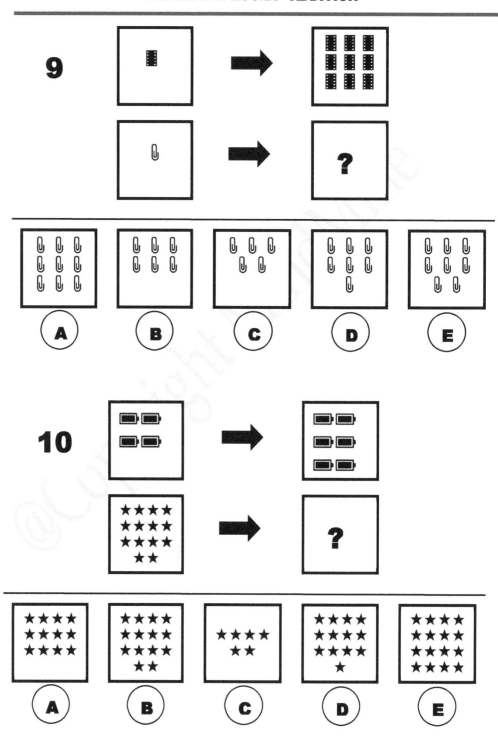

11

A   B   C   D   E

12

A   B   C   D   E

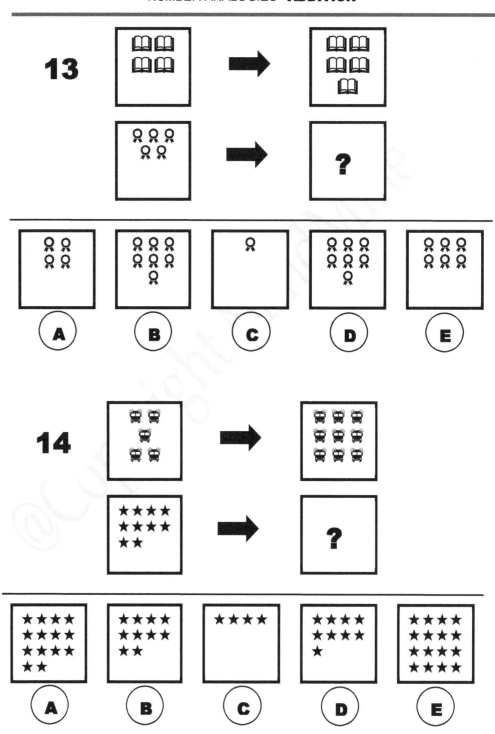

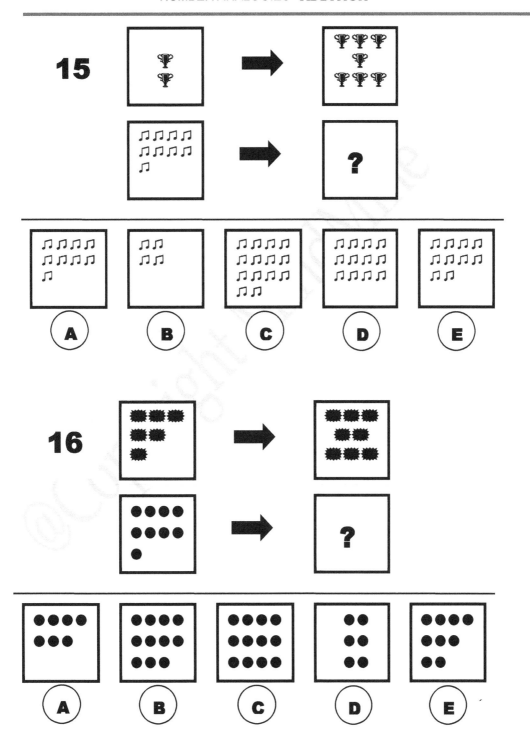

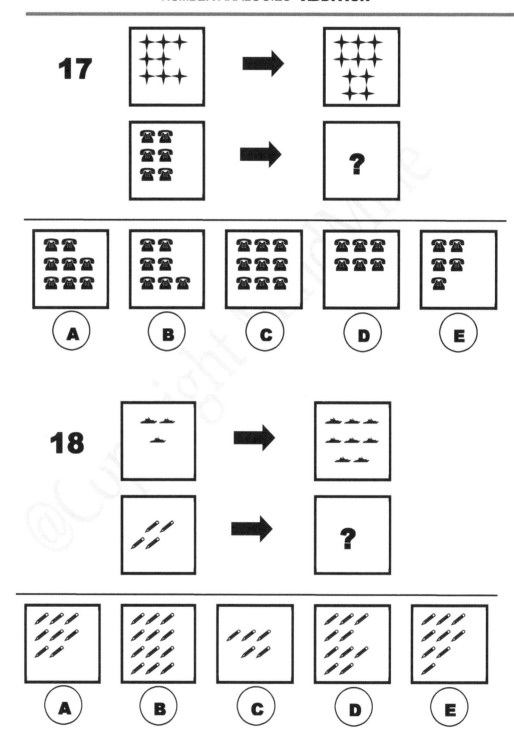

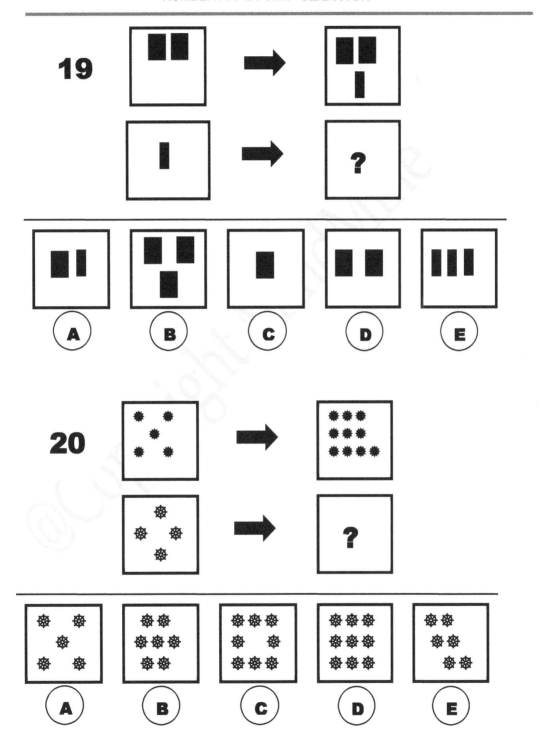

SUBTRACTION

NUMBER ANALOGIES - **Subtraction**

Analogy

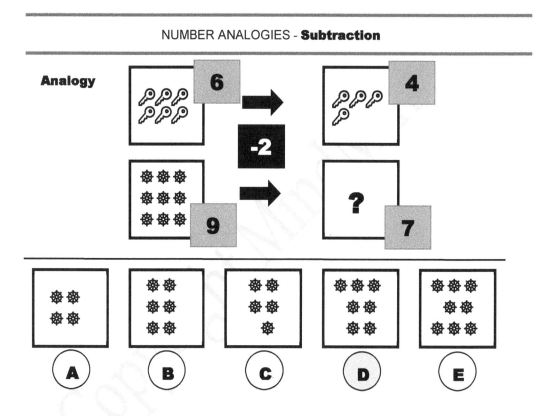

Analogy: Subtract 2   Given 6-**2** = 4   so   9-**2** = 7   **Answer = D**

NUMBER ANALOGIES - **Subtraction**

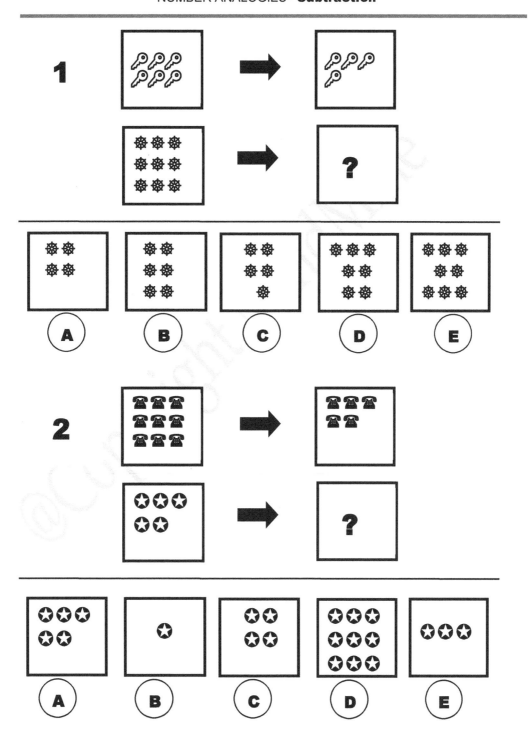

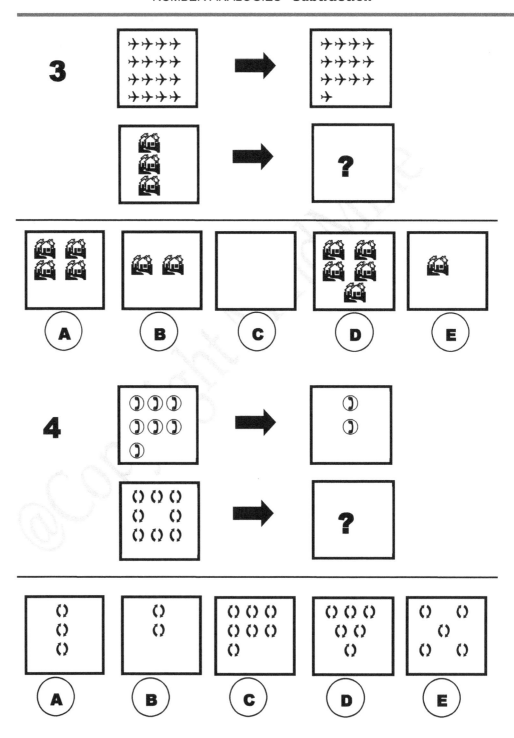

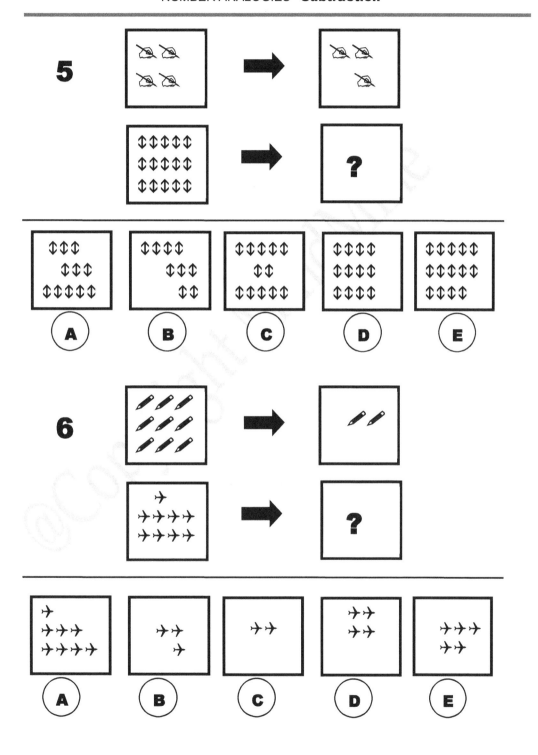

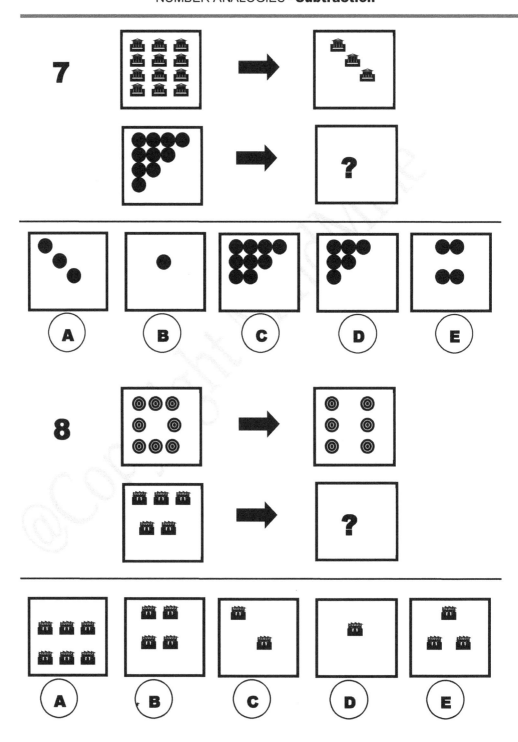

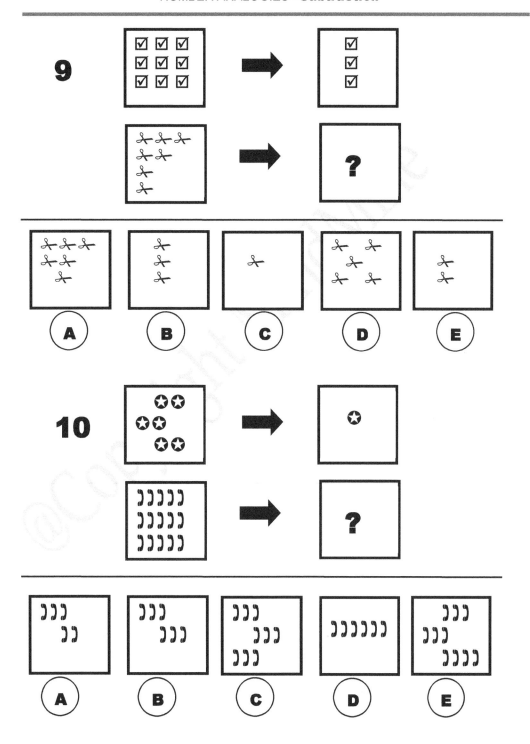

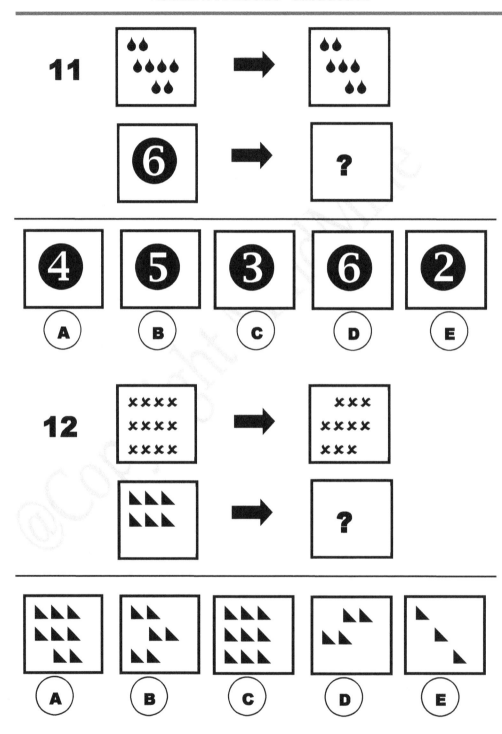

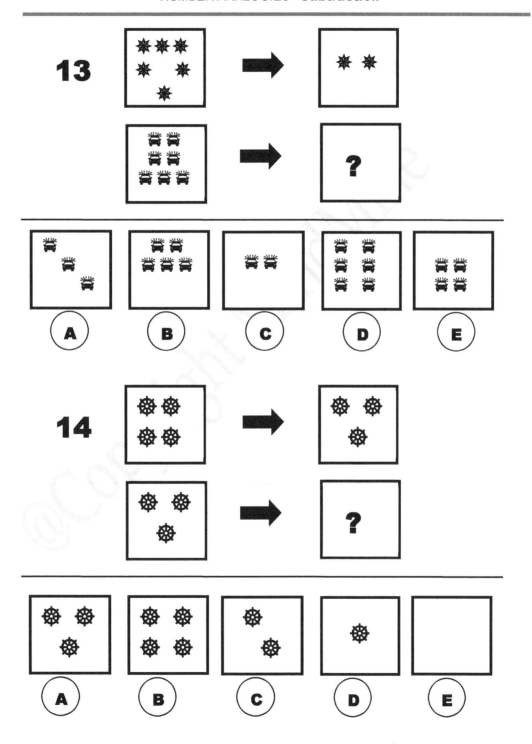

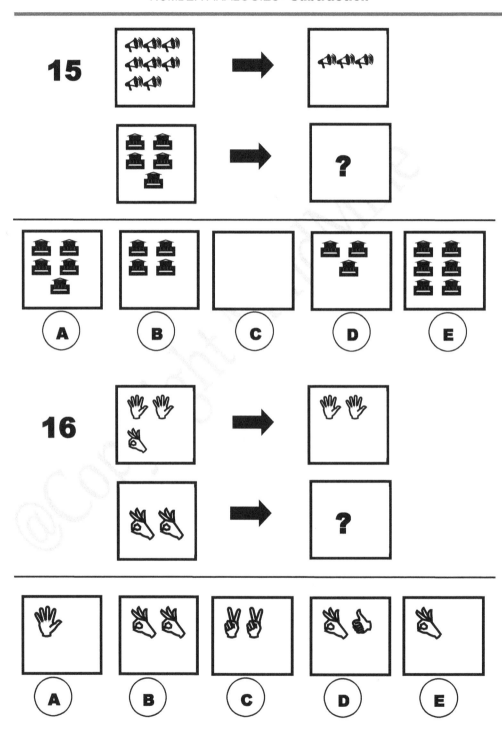

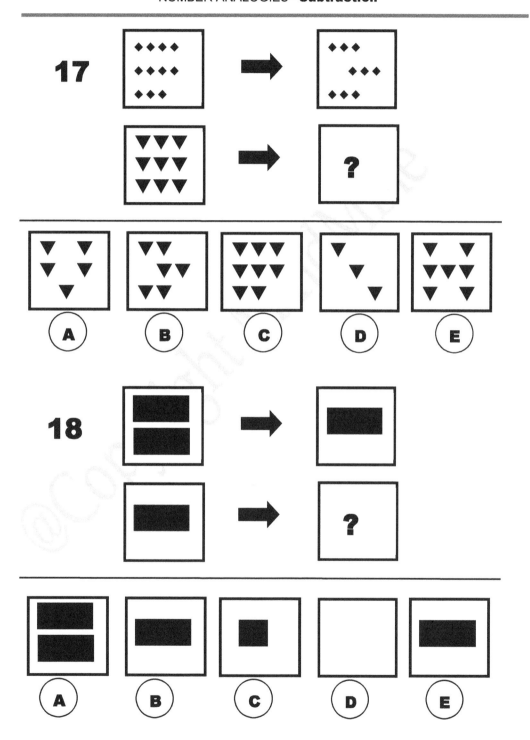

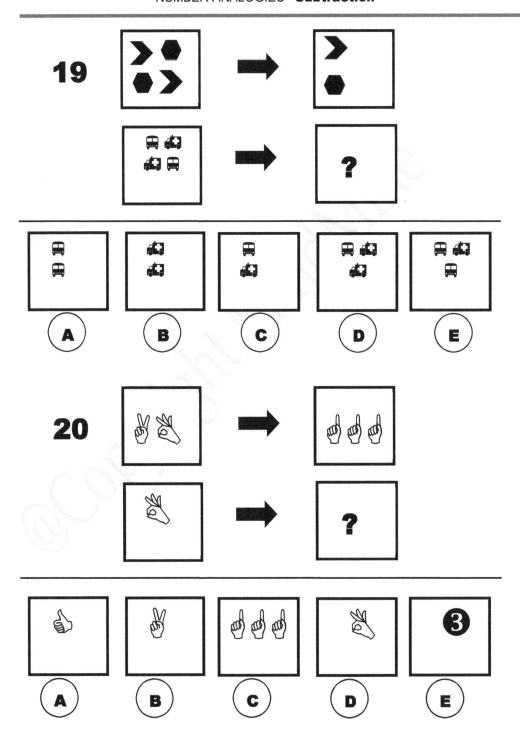

MULTIPLICATION

NUMBER ANALOGIES - **Multiplication**

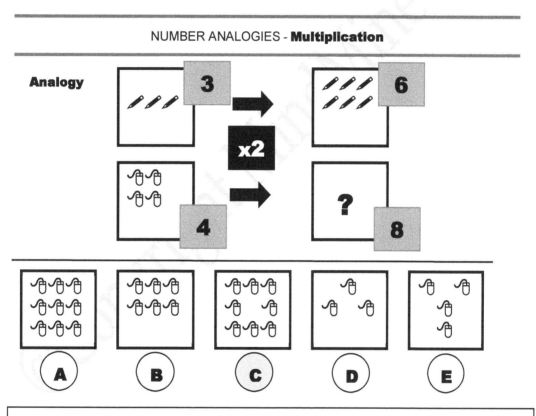

Analogy

| | | A | B | C | D | E |

Analogy: Multiply by 2   Given 3**X2** = 6 so 4**X2** = 8   **Answer = C**

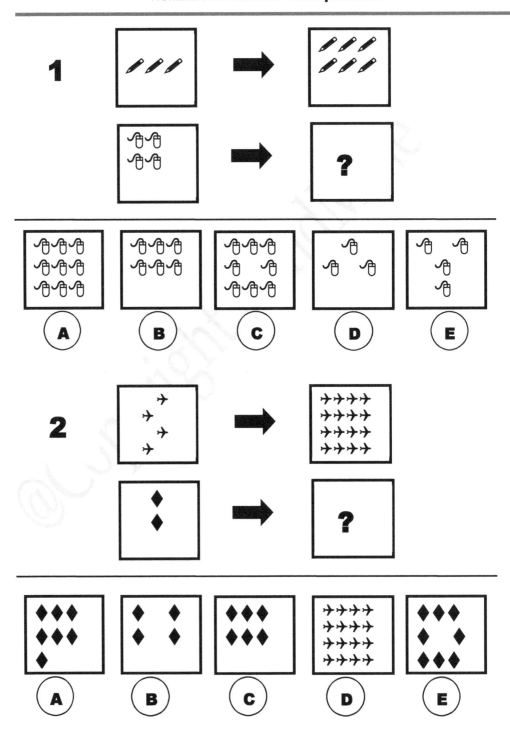

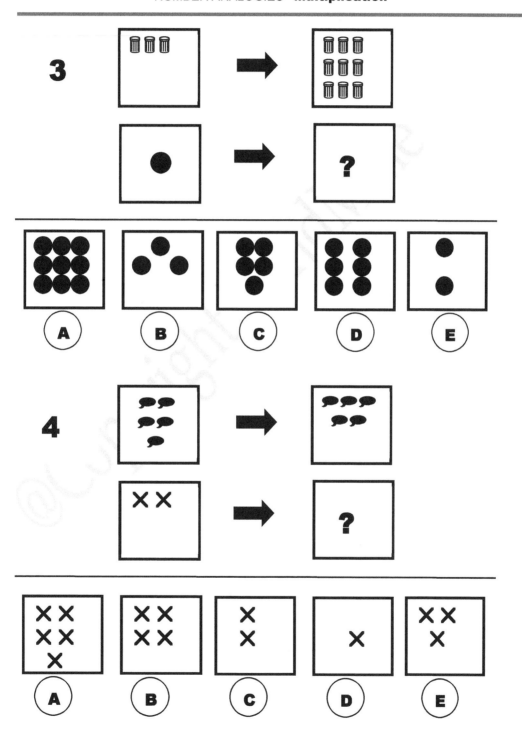

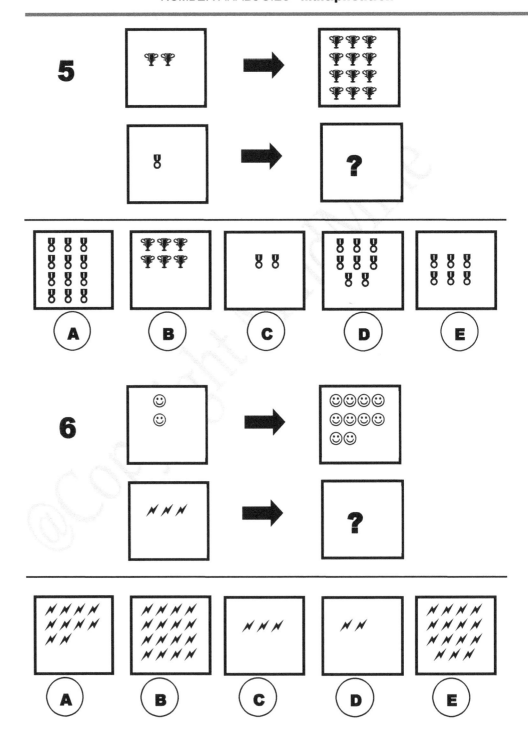

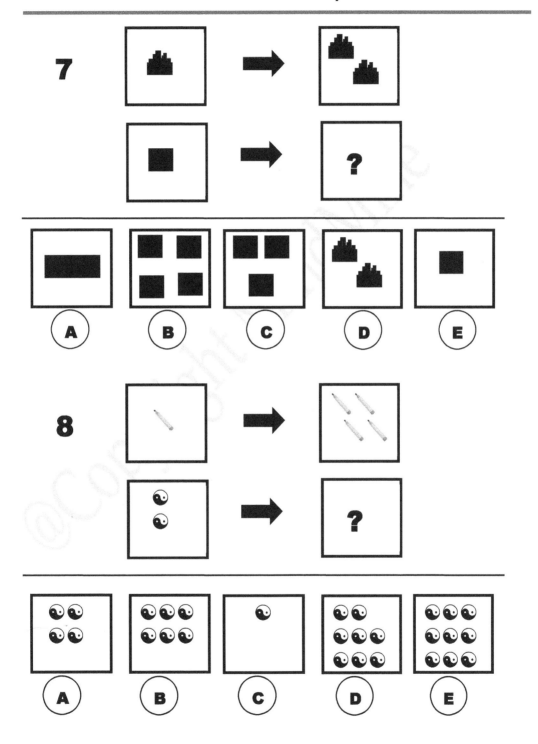

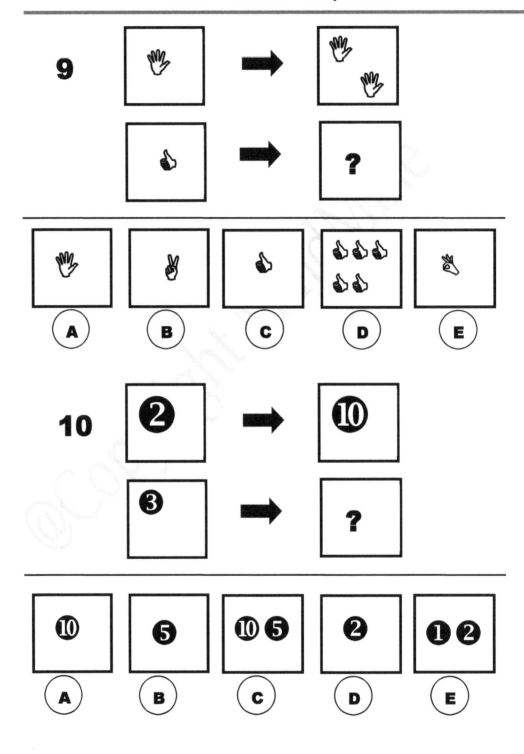

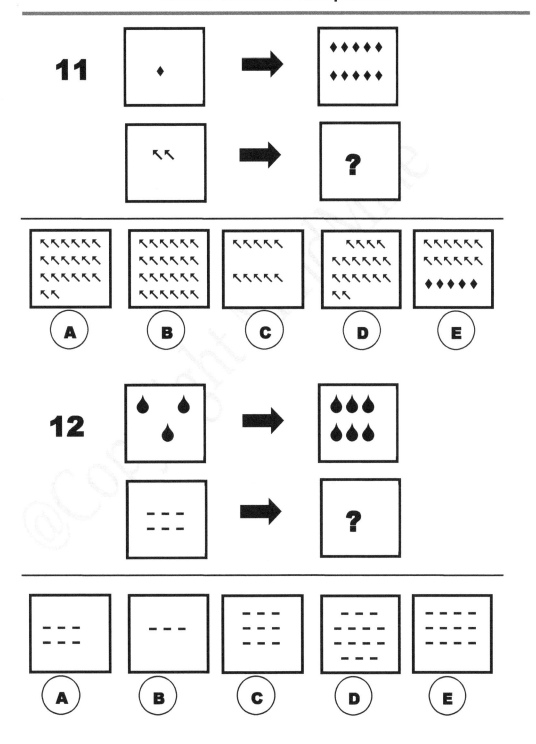

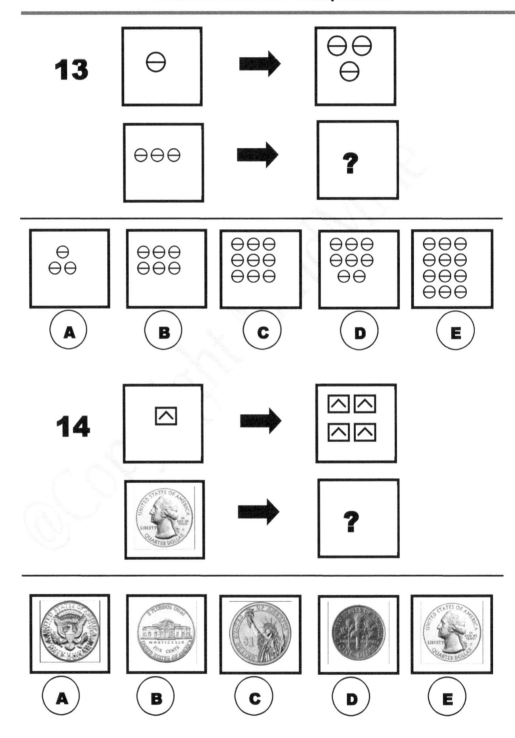

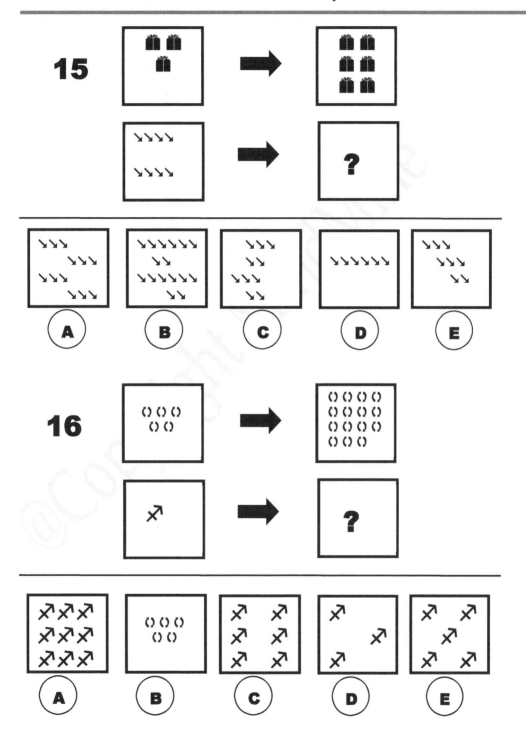

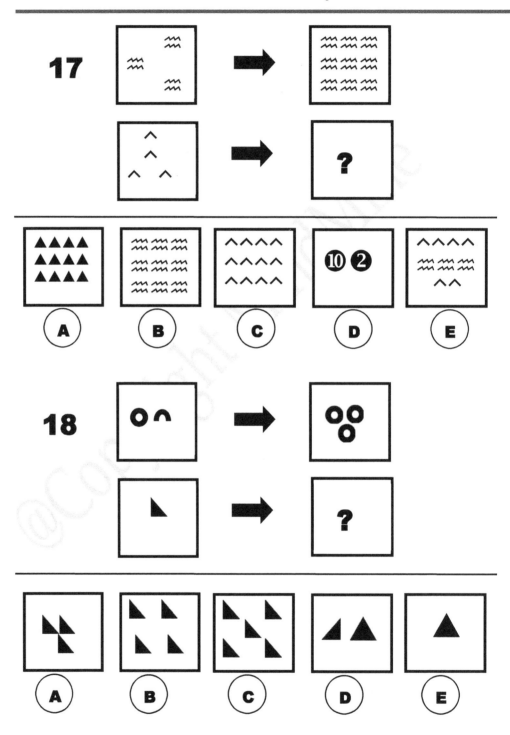

NUMBER ANALOGIES - **Multiplication**

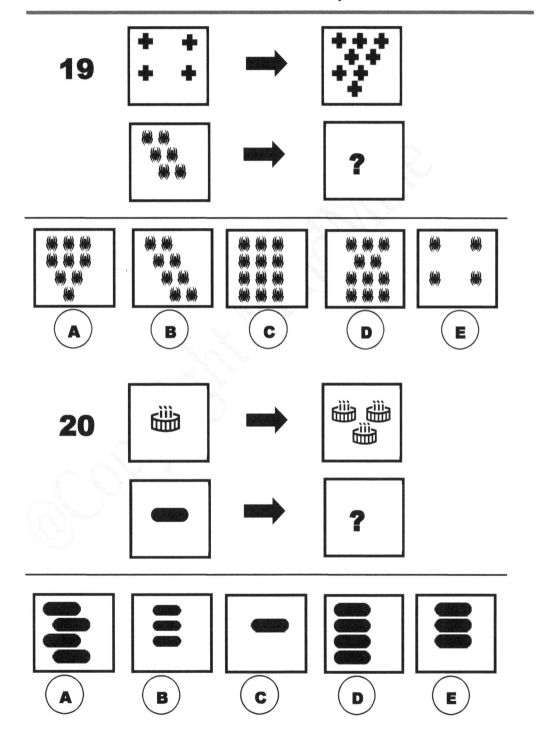

DIVISION

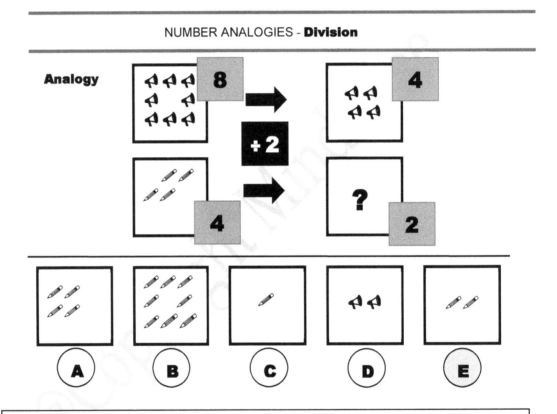

Analogy: Divide by 2   Given 8÷**2** = 4 so 4÷**2** = 2   **Answer = E**

(Half of 8 is 4 so Half of 4 is 2)

Analogy

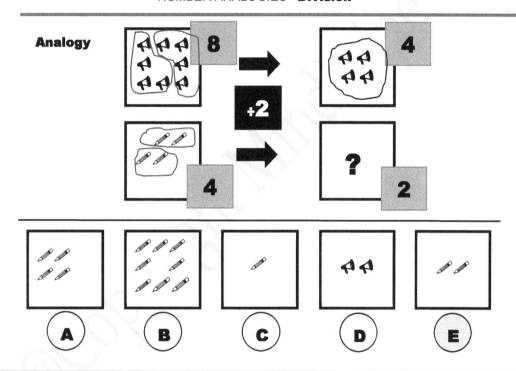

Solving Divisions using Groupings:

2 Groups of Four Horns becomes 1 Group of Four Horns

2 Groups of TWO Pencils becomes 1 Group of Two Pencils

Answer is TWO PENCILS

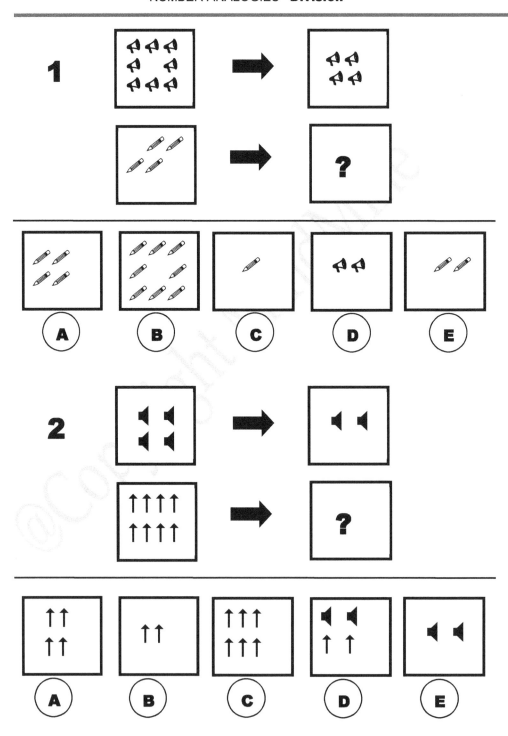

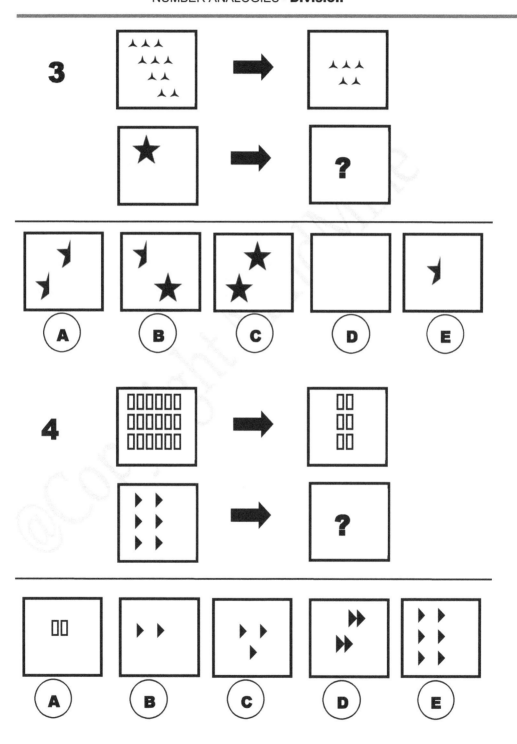

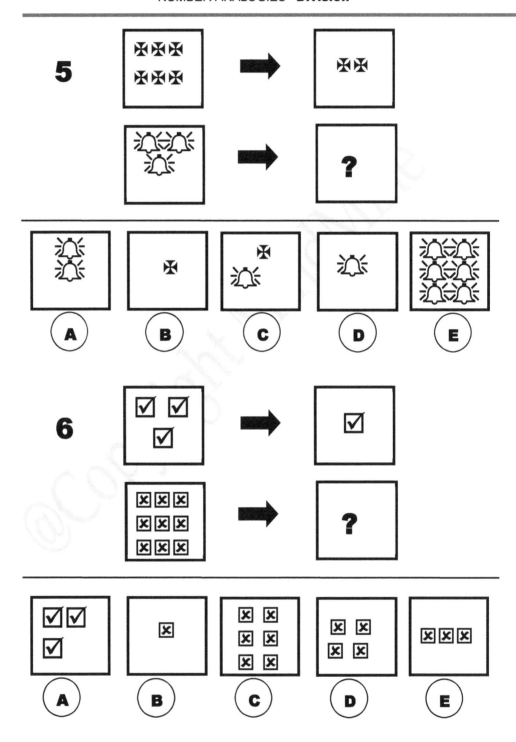

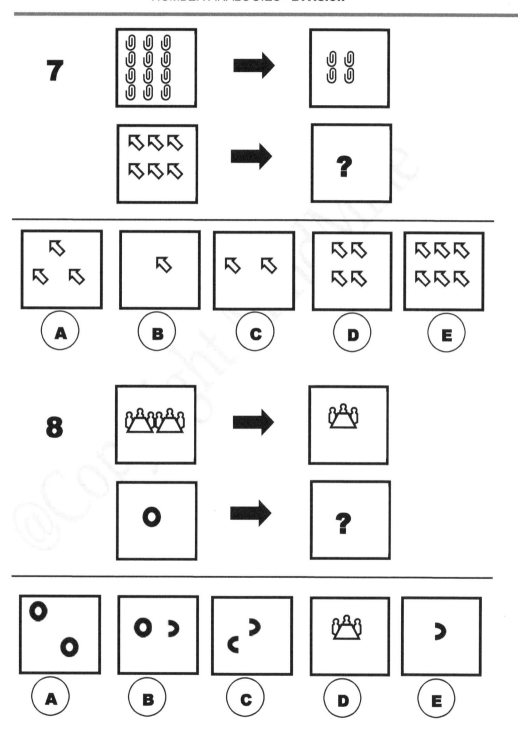

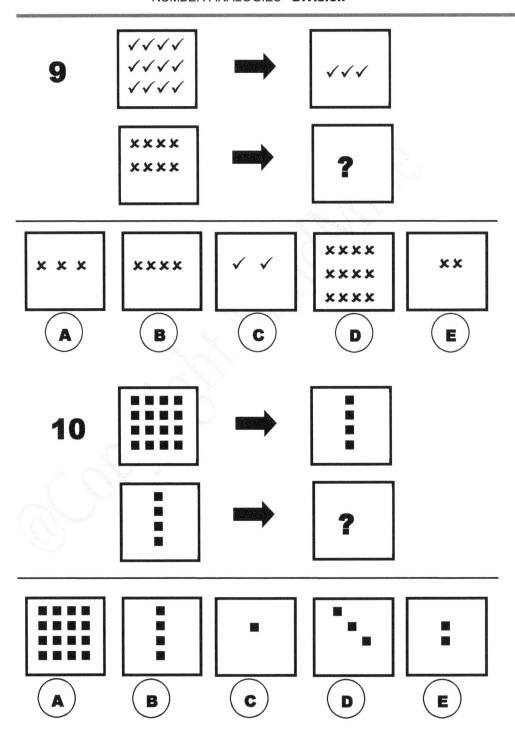

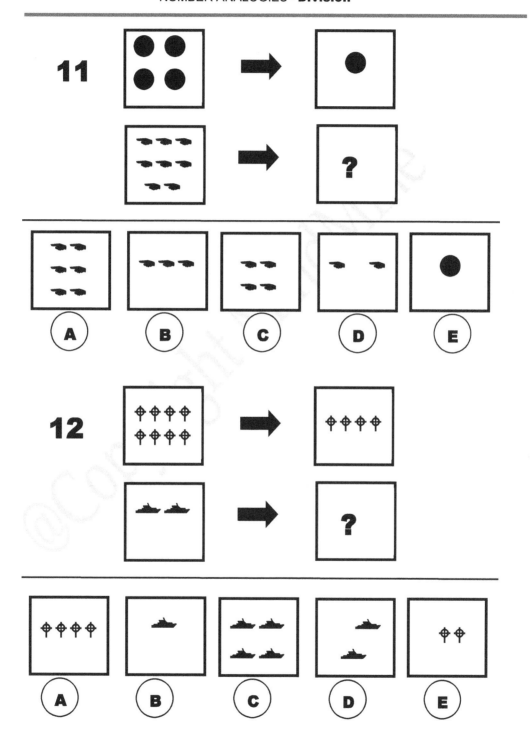

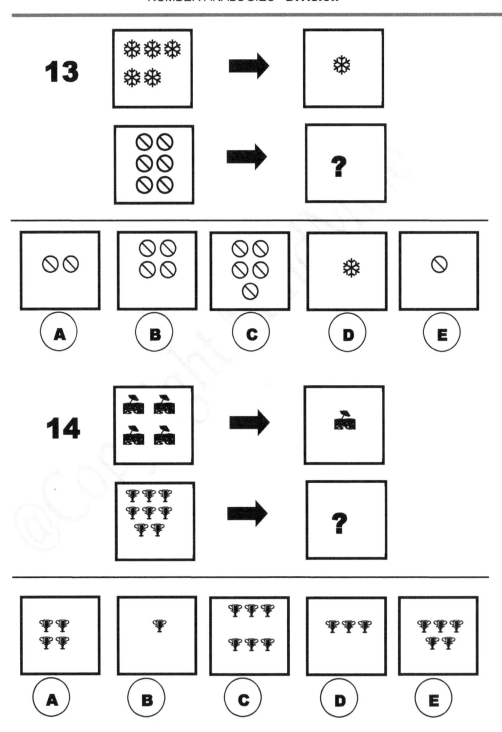

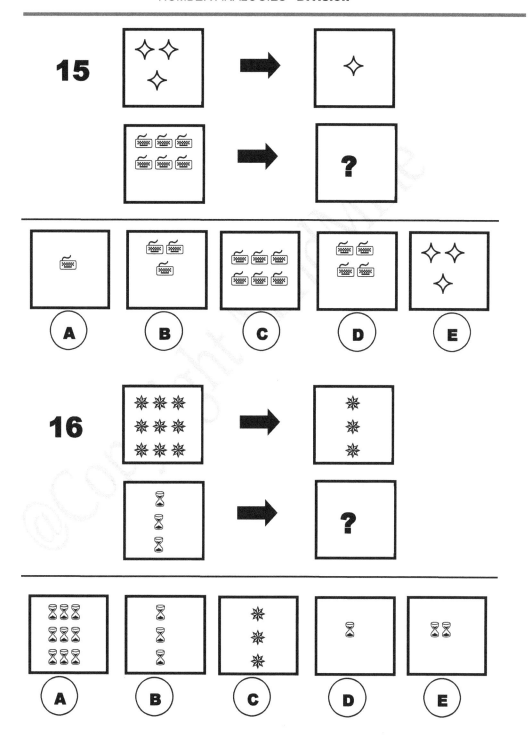

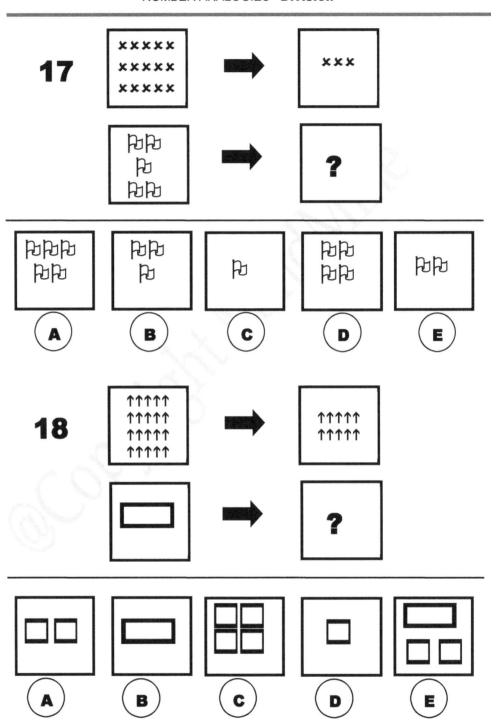

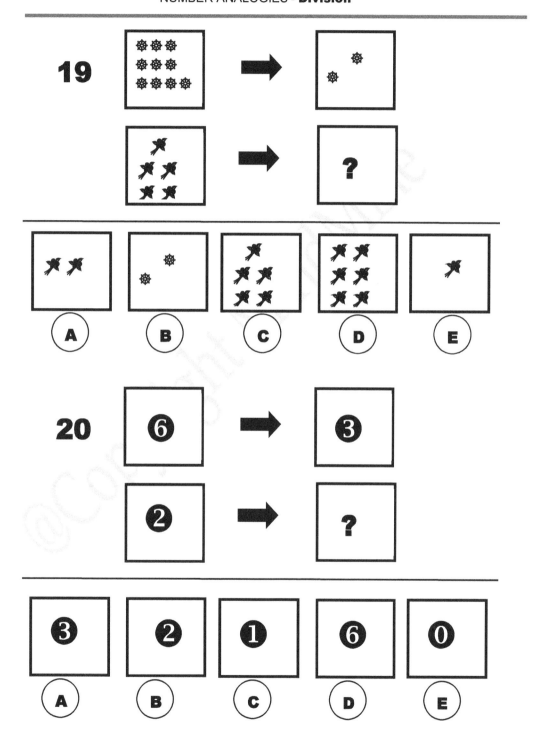

FRACTIONS

NUMBER ANALOGIES - **Fractions**

Analogy

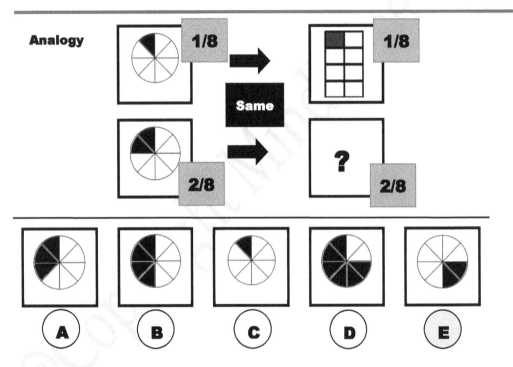

Analogy: Same Fractional Value

Given: 1 out of 8 = 1 out of 8   **So** 2 out of 8 = 2 out of 8

Answer = E

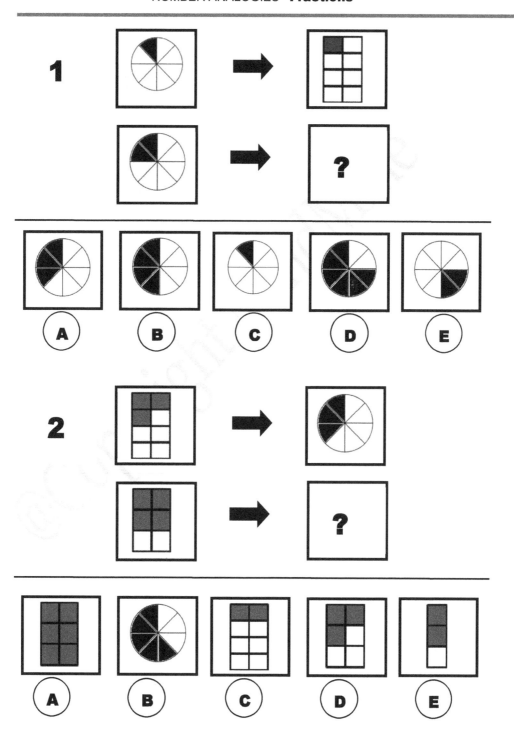

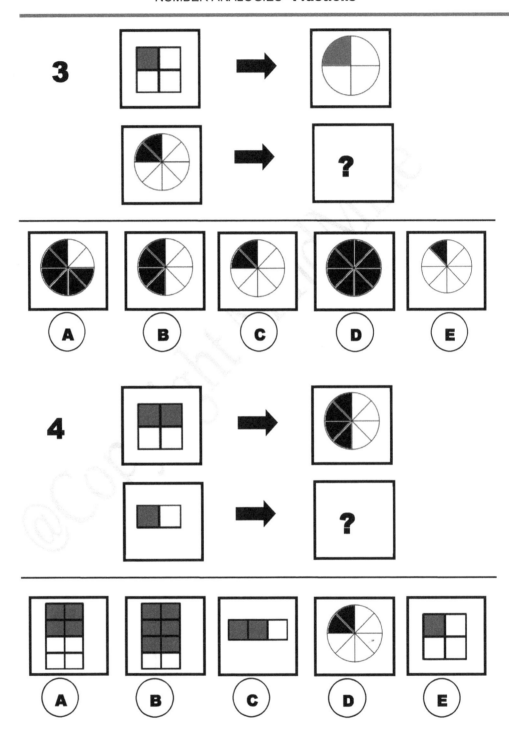

Analogy

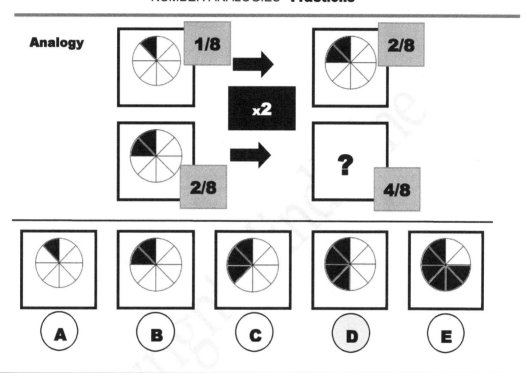

Analogy: Multiplying Fractions with 2

Given: 1 out of 8 = 2 out of 8   **So** 2 out of 8 = 4 out of 8

Note: 4 out of 8 is Same as Half of the whole picture

Answer = D

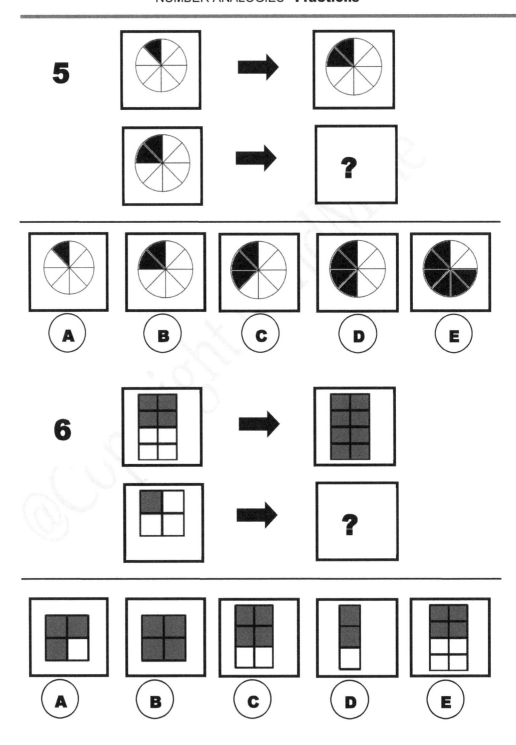

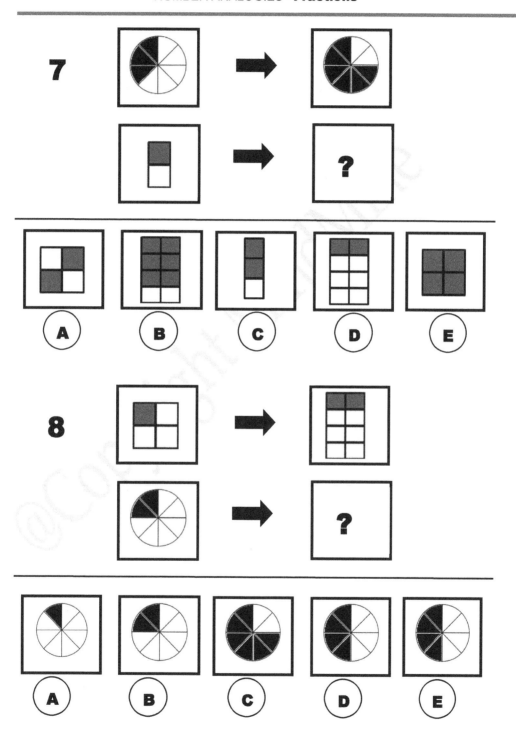

Analogy

2/8	1/8

Half

4/8	?
	2/8

A   B   C   D   E

Analogy: Dividing Fractions with 2 (Half of a given fraction)

Given: 2 out of 8 = 1 out of 8   **So** 4 out of 8 = 2 out of 8

Note: 2 out of 8 is Same as 1 out of 4

Answer = B

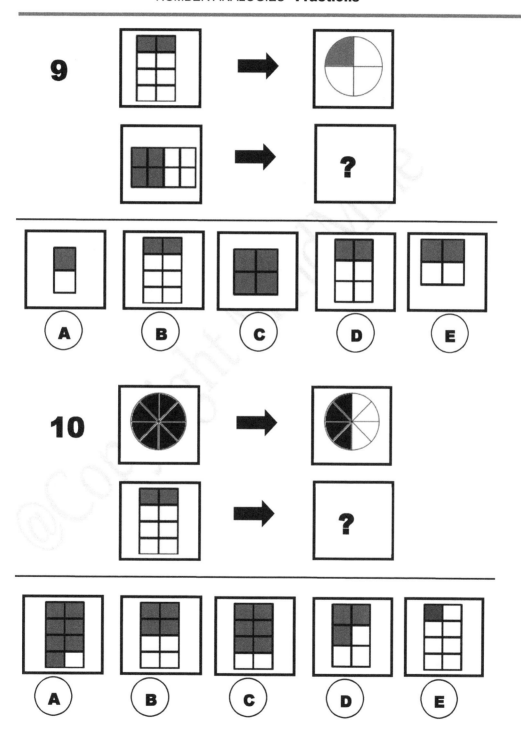

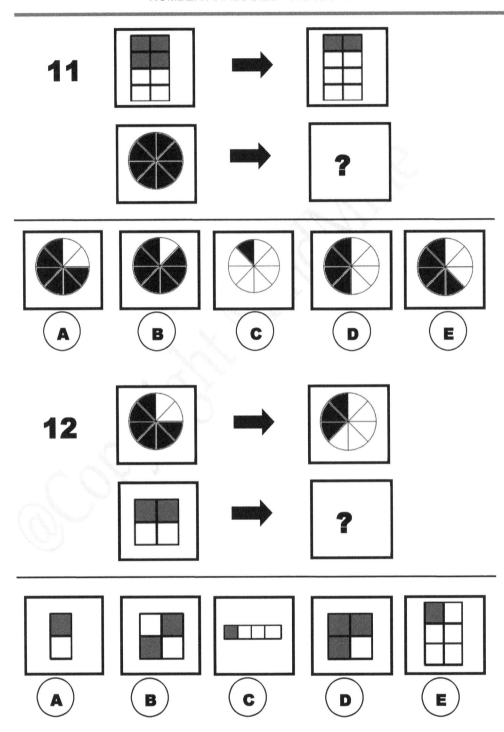

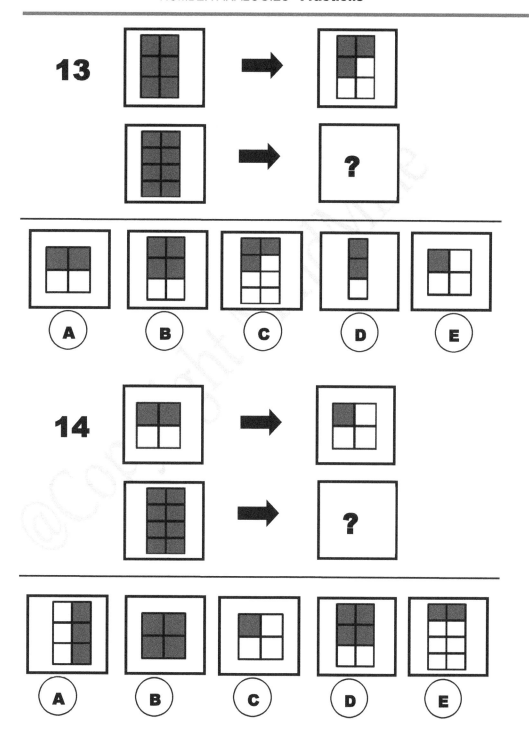

Analogy

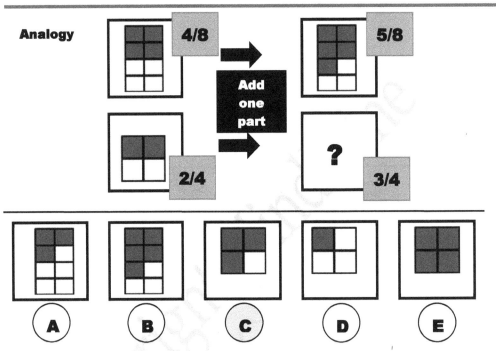

Analogy: Add a part to Fraction

Given: 4 out of 8 = 5 out of 8   **So** 2 out of 4 = 3 out of 4

Answer = C

Analogy

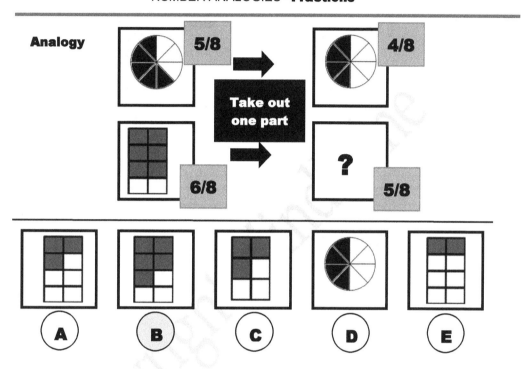

Analogy: Take out one part from Fraction

Given: 5 out of 8 = 4 out of 8   **So** 6 out of 8 = 5 out of 8

Answer = B

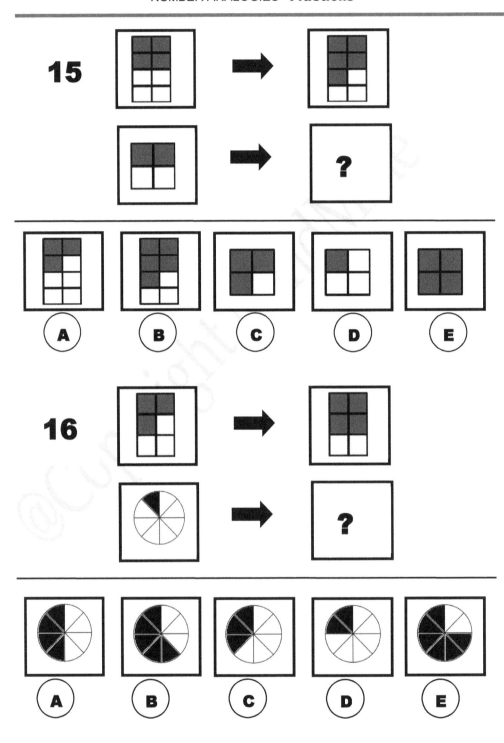

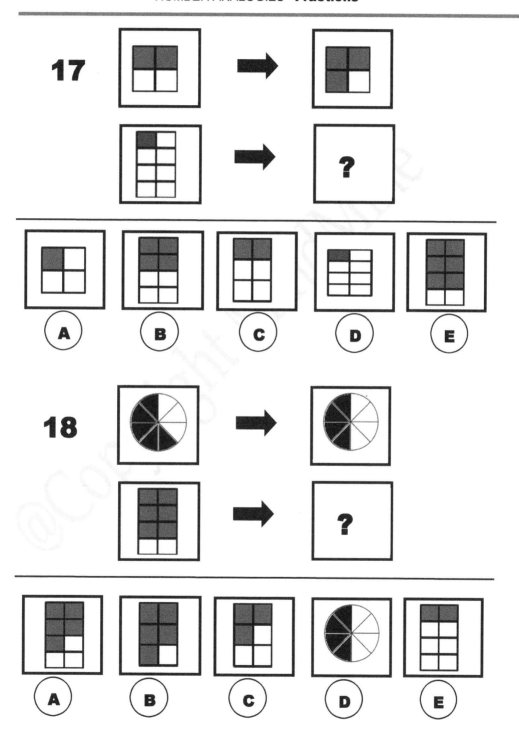

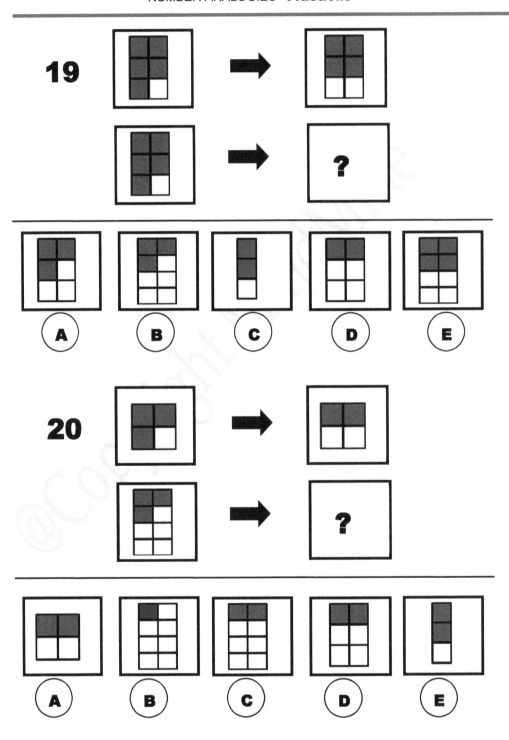

Addition

or

Multiplication

Analogy

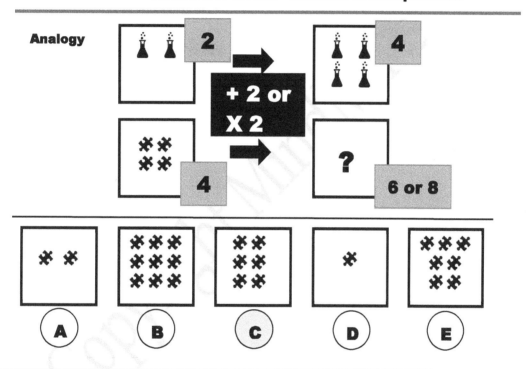

Analogy: Add 2 (OR) Multiply by 2

Given: 2+2 = 4 so 4+2 = 6 (OR)

2x2 = 4 so 4x2 = 8   So Answer is 6 or 8

Answer = C

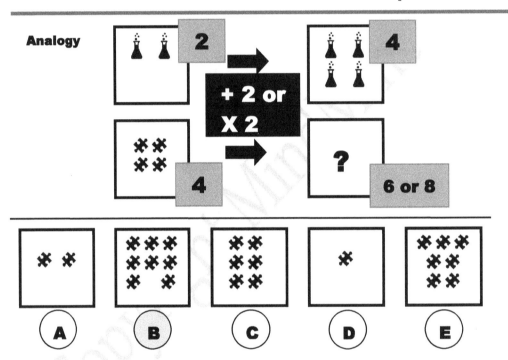

Analogy: Add 2 (OR) Multiply by 2

Given: 2**+2** = 4 so 4**+2** = 6 (OR)

2**x2** = 4 so 4**x2** = 8   So Answer is 6 or 8

Answer = B

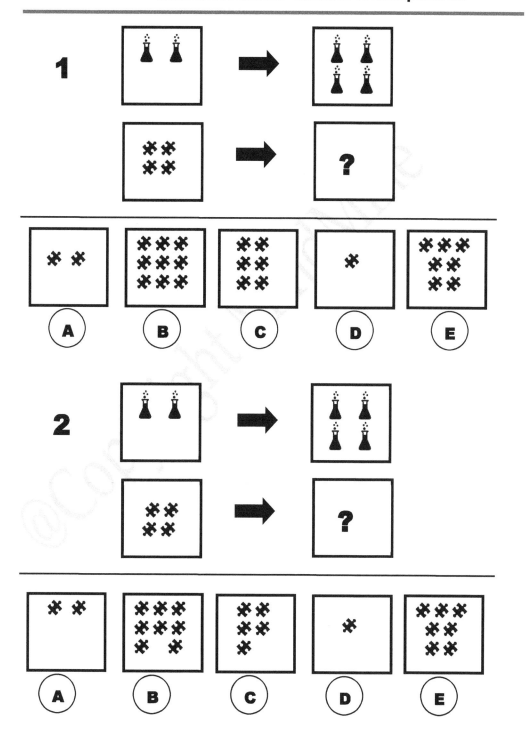

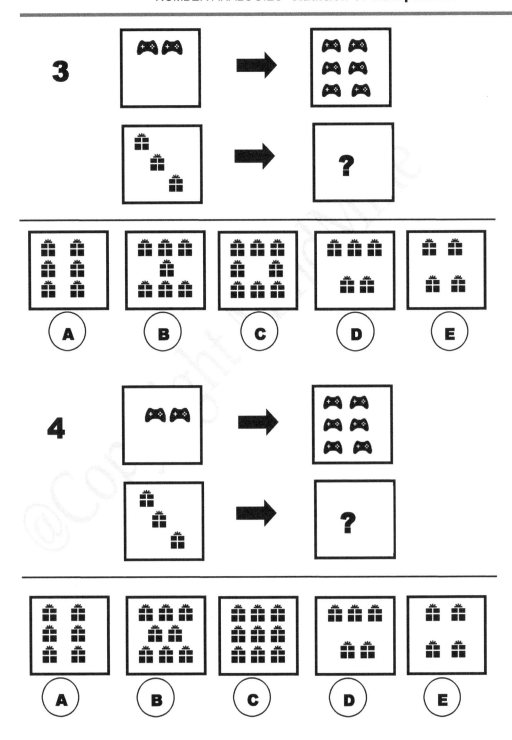

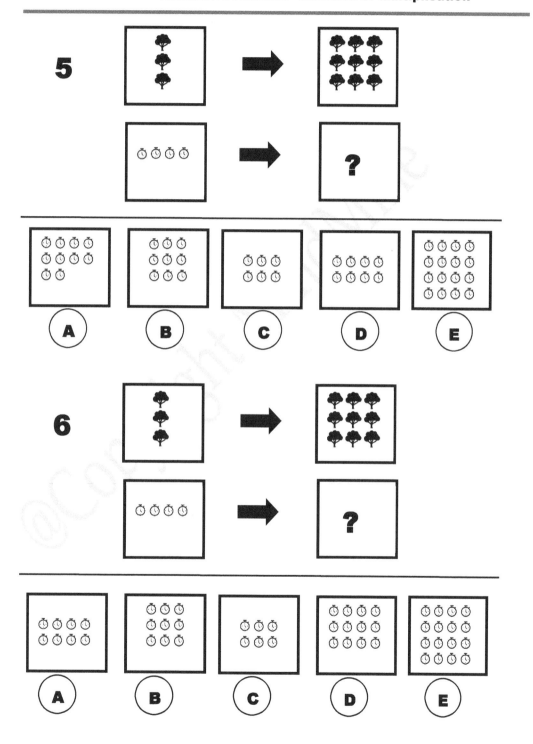

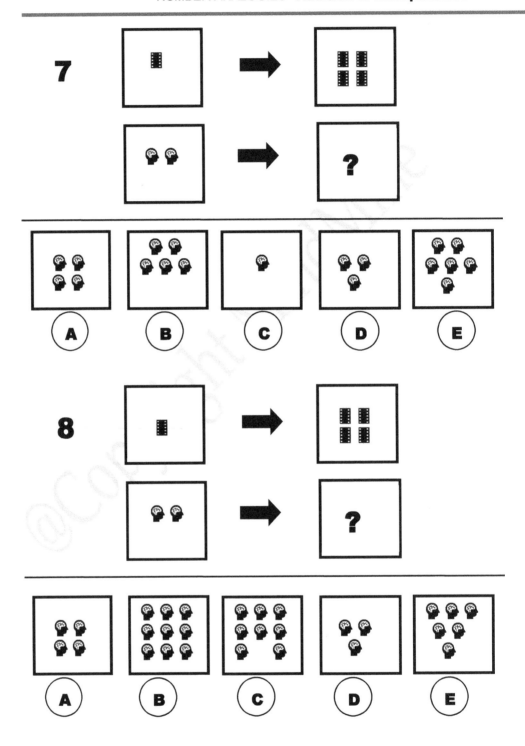

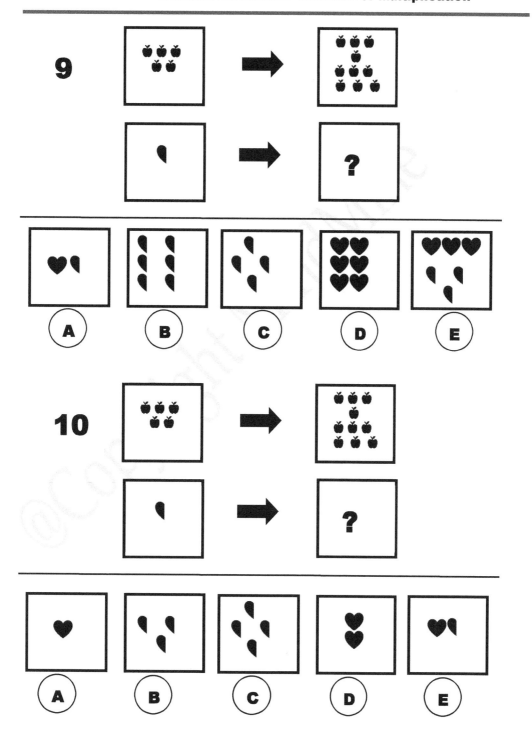

Subtraction

or

Division

Analogy

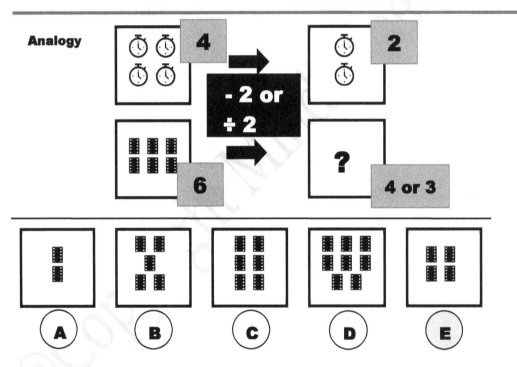

Analogy: Subtract 2 (OR) Divide by 2 (Make Half)
Given: 4-**2** = 2 so 6-**2** = 4 (OR)
    4÷**2** = 2 so 6÷**2** = 3   So Answer is 4 or 3
Answer = E

Analogy

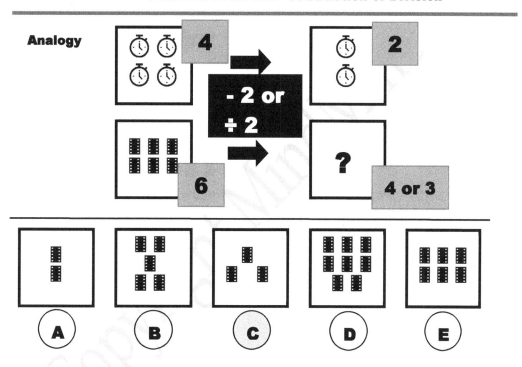

Analogy: Subtract 2 (OR) Divide by 2 (Make Half)

Given: 4-**2** = 2 so 6-**2** = 4 (OR)

4÷**2** = 2 so 6÷**2** = 3   So Answer is 4 or 3

Answer = C

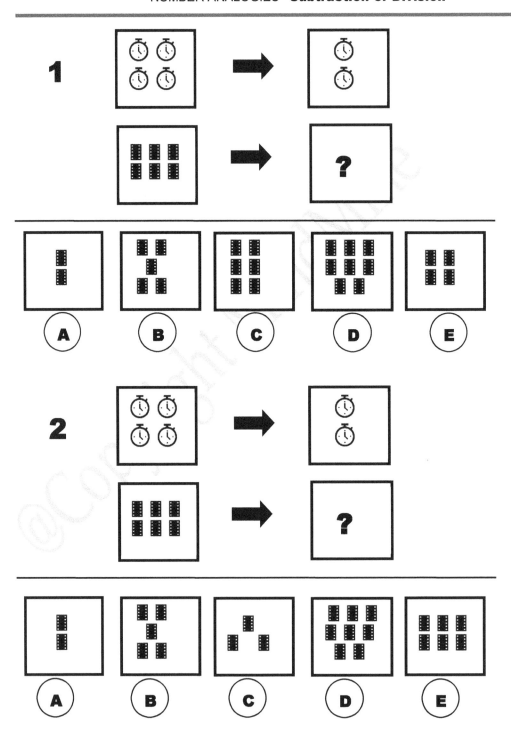

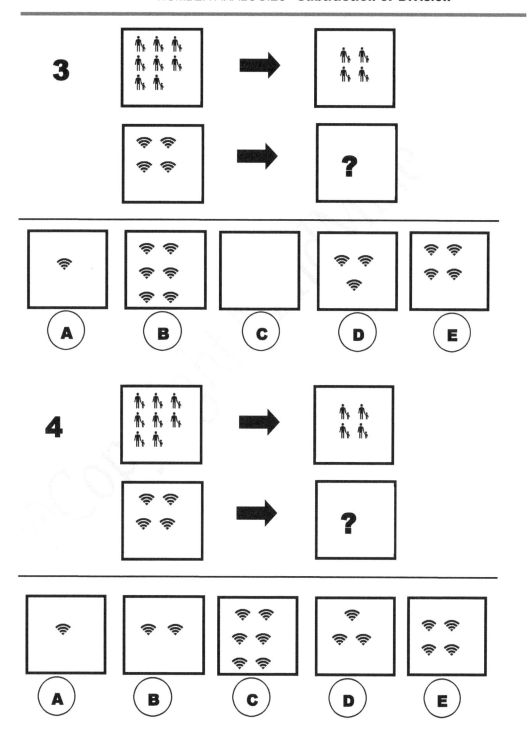

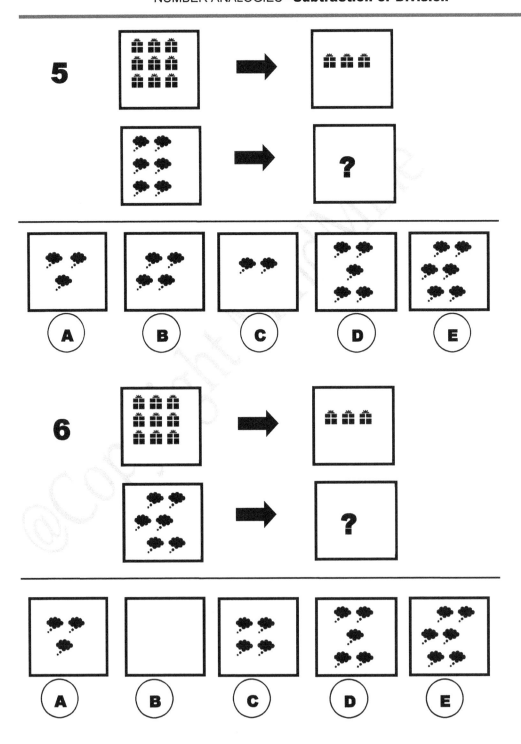

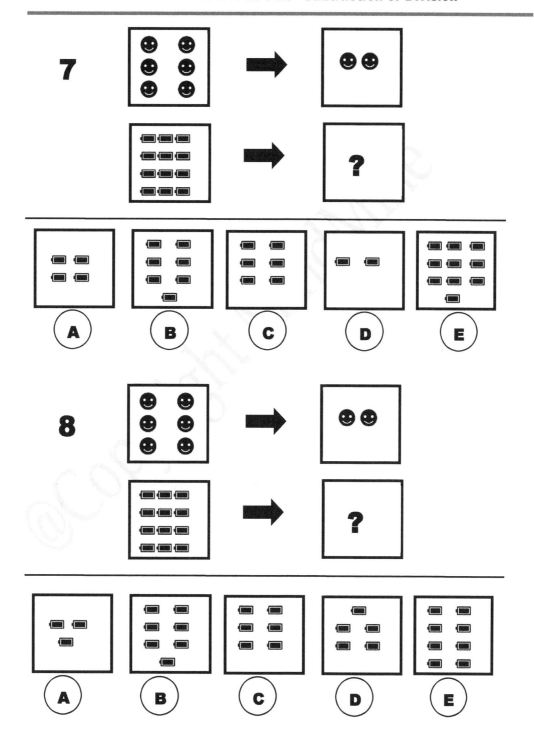

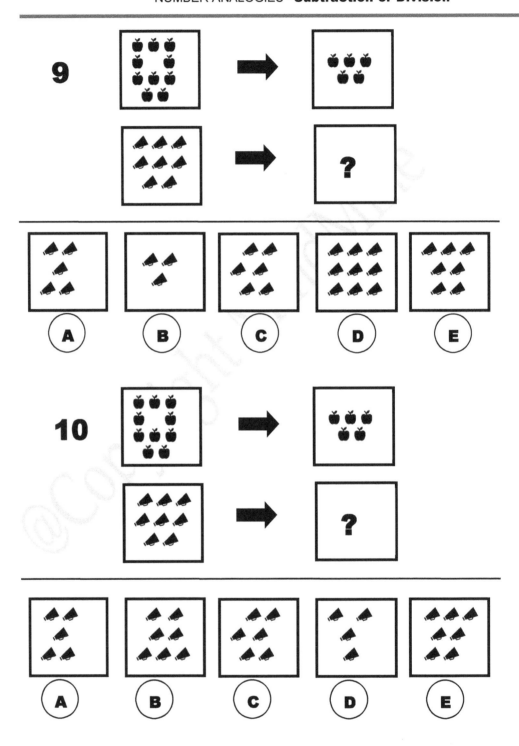

Practice Test

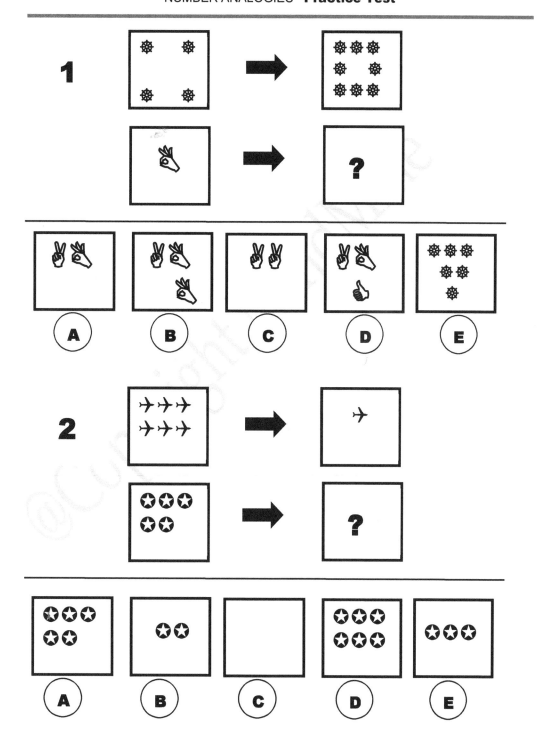

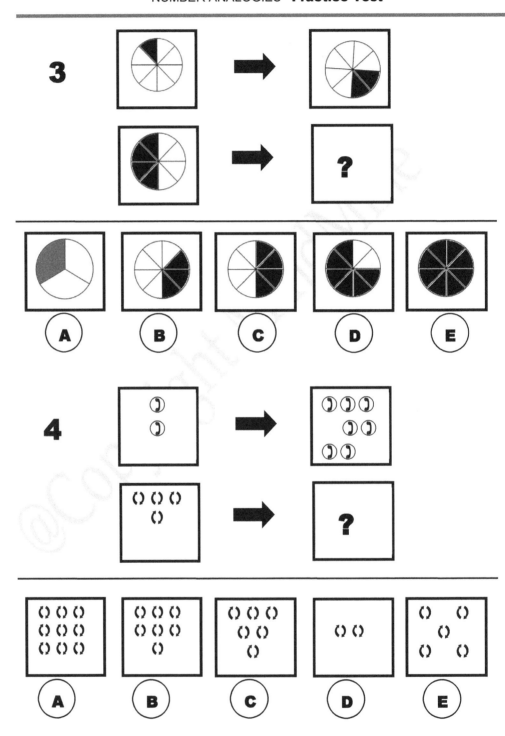

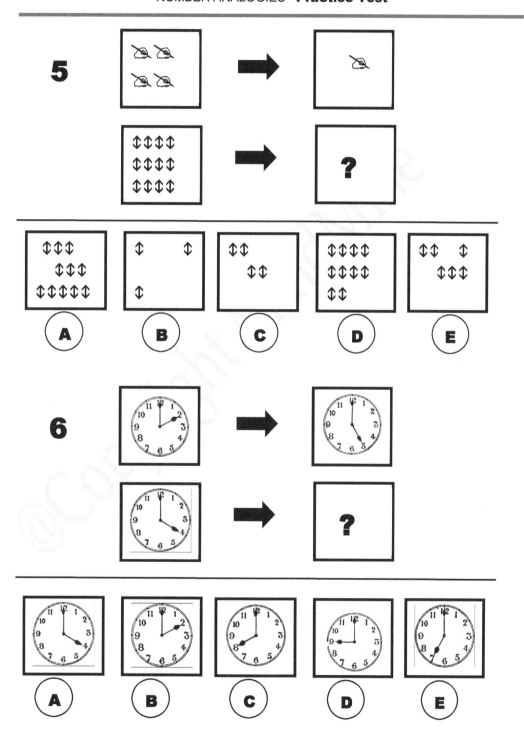

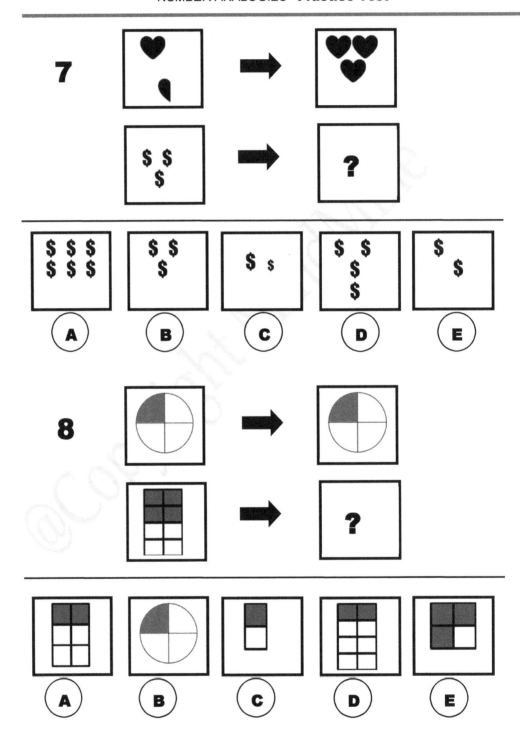

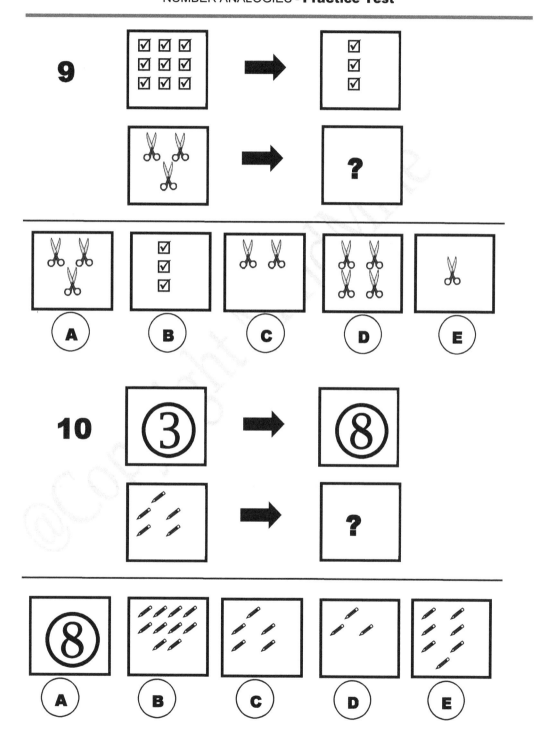

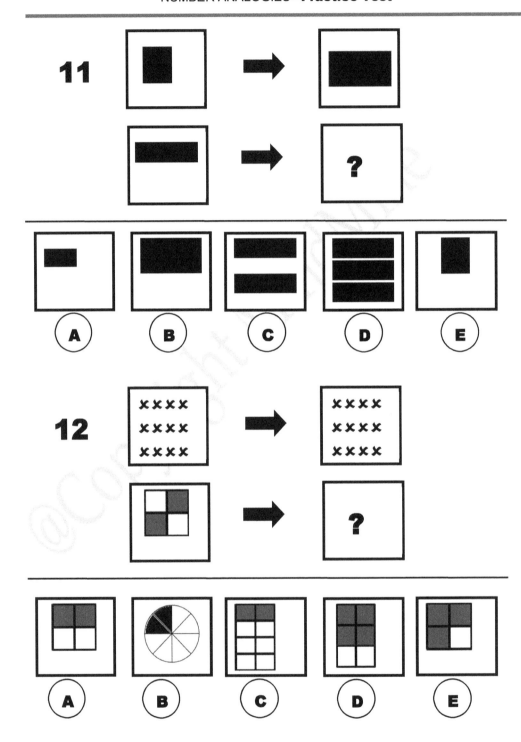

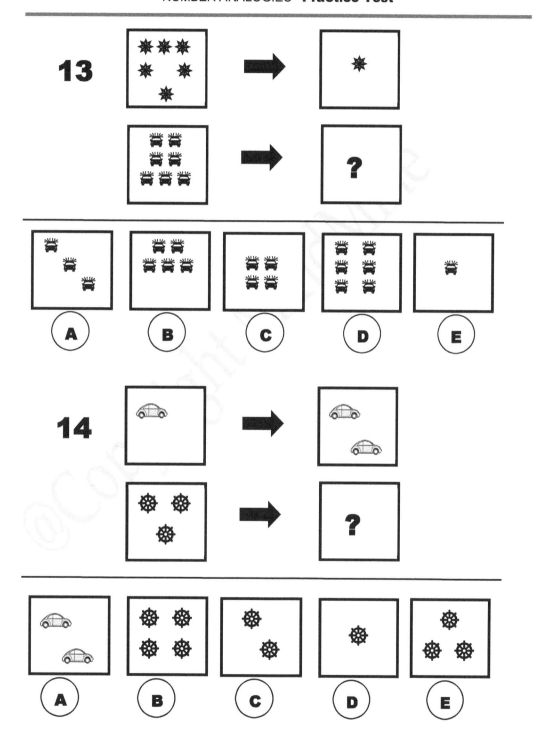

15

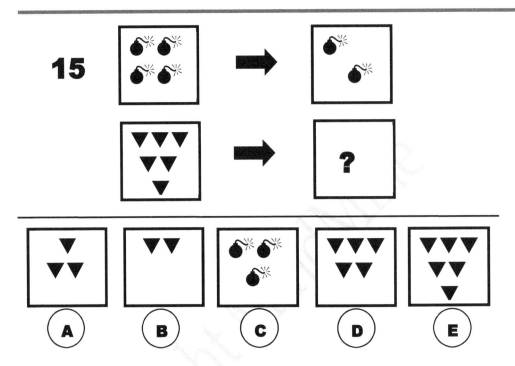

PRACTICE TEST - NUMBER ANALOGIES

1. Ⓐ Ⓑ Ⓒ Ⓓ Ⓔ
2. Ⓐ Ⓑ Ⓒ Ⓓ Ⓔ
3. Ⓐ Ⓑ Ⓒ Ⓓ Ⓔ
4. Ⓐ Ⓑ Ⓒ Ⓓ Ⓔ
5. Ⓐ Ⓑ Ⓒ Ⓓ Ⓔ
6. Ⓐ Ⓑ Ⓒ Ⓓ Ⓔ
7. Ⓐ Ⓑ Ⓒ Ⓓ Ⓔ
8. Ⓐ Ⓑ Ⓒ Ⓓ Ⓔ
9. Ⓐ Ⓑ Ⓒ Ⓓ Ⓔ
10. Ⓐ Ⓑ Ⓒ Ⓓ Ⓔ
11. Ⓐ Ⓑ Ⓒ Ⓓ Ⓔ
12. Ⓐ Ⓑ Ⓒ Ⓓ Ⓔ
13. Ⓐ Ⓑ Ⓒ Ⓓ Ⓔ
14. Ⓐ Ⓑ Ⓒ Ⓓ Ⓔ
15. Ⓐ Ⓑ Ⓒ Ⓓ Ⓔ

ANSWERS

NUMBER ANALOGIES

ADDITIONS

QUESTION	ANSWER	ANALOGY			
1	D	1	+ 3	4	
		4		7	
2	C	3	+ 1	4	
		6		7	
3	B	5	+ 4	9	
		8		12	
4	E	2	+ 7	9	
		5		12	
5	C	10	+ 2	12	
		3		5	

QUESTION	ANSWER		ANALOGY	
6	E	1	**+ 6**	7
		10		16
7	D	2	**+ 4**	6
		6		10
8	A	1	**+ 5**	6
		5		10
9	A	1	**+ 8**	9
		1		9
10	E	4	**+ 2**	6
		14		16

QUESTION	ANSWER		ANALOGY	
11	B	9 7	+ 3	12 10
12	E	6 8	+ 6	12 14
13	E	4 5	+ 1	5 6
14	A	5 10	+ 4	9 14
15	C	2 9	+ 5	7 14

QUESTION	ANSWER		ANALOGY	
16	B	6	+ 2	8
		9		11
17	A	8	+ 2	10
		6		8
18	E	3	+ 5	8
		4		9
19	C	2	+ 1/2	2 1/2
		1/2		1
20	D	5	+ 5	10
		4		9

NUMBER ANALOGIES

SUBTRACTIONS

QUESTION	ANSWER	ANALOGY	
1	D	6 -2	4
		9	7
2	B	9 -4	5
		5	1
3	C	16 -3	13
		3	0
4	A	7 -5	2
		8	3
5	E	4 -1	3
		15	14

QUESTION	ANSWER	ANALOGY			
6	C	9 9	- 7	2 2	
7	B	12 10	- 9	3 1	
8	E	8 5	- 2	6 3	
9	C	9 7	- 6	3 1	
10	E	6 15	- 5	1 10	

QUESTION	ANSWER	ANALOGY		
11	B	8 6	- 1	7 5
12	D	12 6	- 2	10 4
13	A	6 7	- 4	2 3
14	C	4 3	- 1	3 2
15	C	8 5	- 5	3 0

QUESTION	ANSWER	ANALOGY		
16	E	13	- 3	10
		6		3
17	E	11	- 2	9
		9		7
18	D	2	- 1	1
		1		0
19	C	4	- 1 of each picture	2
		4		2
20	A	5	- 2	3
		3		1

NUMBER ANALOGIES

MULTIPLICATIONS

QUESTION	ANSWER	ANALOGY		
1	C	3	$\times 2$	6
		4		8
2	E	4	$\times 4$	16
		2		8
3	B	3	$\times 3$	9
		1		3
4	C	5	$\times 1$	5
		2		2
5	E	2	$\times 6$	12
		1		6

QUESTION	ANSWER	ANALOGY			
6	E	2	**X 5**	10	
		3		15	
7	A	1	**X 2**	2	
		½		1	
8	D	1	**X 4**	4	
		2		8	
9	B	5	**X 2**	10	
		1		2	
10	C	2	**X 5**	10	
		3		15	

QUESTION	ANSWER	ANALOGY	
11	A	1 **X 10** 10	
		2 20	
12	E	3 **X 2** 6	
		6 12	
13	C	1 **X 3** 3	
		3 9	
14	C	1 **X 4** 4	
		25C $1(100C)	
15	B	3 **X 2** 6	
		8 16	

QUESTION	ANSWER	ANALOGY	
16	D	5 X 3 1	15 3
17	C	6 X 3 4	18 12
18	E	1 1/2 X 2 ½	3 1
19	C	4 X 2 6	8 12
20	E	1 X 3 1	3 3

NUMBER ANALOGIES

DIVISIONS

QUESTION	ANSWER	ANALOGY		
1	E	8	$\div 2$	4
		4		2
2	A	4	$\div 2$	2
		8		4
3	E	10	$\div 2$	5
		1		½
4	B	18	$\div 3$	6
		6		2
5	D	6	$\div 3$	2
		3		1

QUESTION	ANSWER	ANALOGY		
6	E	3 9	÷ 3	1 3
7	C	12 6	÷ 3	4 2
8	E	2 1	÷ 2	1 ½
9	E	12 8	÷ 4	3 2
10	C	16 4	÷ 4	4 1

QUESTION	ANSWER		ANALOGY	
11	D	4	$\div 4$	1
		8		2
12	B	8	$\div 2$	4
		2		1
13	E	5	$\div$ WITH SAME NUMBER	1
		6		1
14	B	4	$\div$ WITH SAME NUMBER	1
		8		1
15	A	3	$\div$ WITH SAME NUMBER	1
		6		1

QUESTION	ANSWER	ANALOGY	
16	D	9 3	$\div 3$	3 1
17	C	15 5	$\div 5$	3 1
18	D	20 1	$\div 2$	10 ½
19	E	10 5	$\div 5$	2 1
20	C	6 2	$\div 2$	3 1

NUMBER ANALOGIES

Fractions

QUESTION	ANSWER		ANALOGY	
1	E	1/8	**Same**	1/8
		2/8		2/8
2	E	3/8	**Same**	3/8
		4/6		4/6 or 2/3
3	C	¼	**Same**	¼
		2/8		2/8 or 1/4
4	A	2/4	**Same**	4/8 or 2/4
		½		½ or 4/8
5	D	1/8	**X 2**	2/8
		2/8		4/8

QUESTION	ANSWER	ANALOGY		
6	E	4/8	X 2	8/8
		¼		2/4 or ½ or 4/8
7	E	3/8	X 2	6/8
		½		2/2 or Full
8	B	¼	Same	2/8 or 1/4
		2/8		2/8
9	E	2/8	Same	1/4
		4/8		4/8 or 2/4 or 1/2
10	E	8/8	÷ 2	4/8
		2/8		1/8

QUESTION	ANSWER	ANALOGY		
11	D	4/8 8/8	÷ 2	2/8 4/8
12	C	6/8 2/4	÷ 2	3/8 1/4
13	A	6/6 8/8	÷ 2	3/6 4/8 or 2/4
14	A	2/4 8/8	÷ 2	1/4 4/8 or Half
15	C	4/8 2/4	+ 1 part	5/8 3/4

QUESTION	ANSWER		ANALOGY	
16	D	3/6	+ 1	4/6
		1/8	part	2/8
17	A	2/4	+ 1	3/4
		1/8	part	2/8 or 1/4
18	A	5/8	- 1	4/8
		6/8	part	5/8
19	C	5/6	- 1	4/6
		5/6	part	4/6 or 2/3
20	C	¾	- 1	2/4
		3/8	part	2/8

NUMBER ANALOGIES

Additions or Multiplications

QUESTION	ANSWER	ANALOGY	
1	C	2 $+2$ 4	4 6
2	B	2 $\times 2$ 4	4 8
3	B	2 $+4$ 3	6 7
4	C	2 $\times 3$ 3	6 9
5	A	3 $+6$ 4	9 10

QUESTION ANSWER		ANALOGY		
6	D	3	x 3	9
		4		12
7	B	1	+ 3	4
		2		5
8	C	1	X 4	4
		2		8
9	B	5	+ 5	10
		1		6
10	A	5	X 2	10
		½		1

NUMBER ANALOGIES

Subtractions or Divisions

QUESTION	ANSWER	ANALOGY	
1	E	4 - 2 2	
		6 4	
2	C	4 ÷ 2 2	
		6 3	
3	C	8 - 4 4	
		4 0	
4	B	8 ÷ 2 4	
		4 2	
5	C	9 ÷ 3 3	
		6 2	

QUESTION	ANSWER	ANALOGY			
6	B	9	- 6	3	
		6		0	
7	A	6	÷ 3	2	
		12		4	
8	E	6	- 4	2	
		12		8	
9	B	10	- 5	5	
		8		3	
10	D	10	÷ 2	5	
		8		4	

NUMBER ANALOGIES

PRACTICE TEST

QUESTION	ANSWER
1	D
2	C
3	E
4	A
5	B
6	E
7	A

8	C
9	E
10	B
11	C
12	A
13	E
14	B
15	A

CPSIA information can be obtained
at www.ICGtesting.com
Printed in the USA
LVHW060200180219
607850LV00014B/260/P

9 781983 40